Firebirds

ERIC ETHAN

Gareth Stevens Publishing
MILWAUKEE

For a free color catalog describing Gareth Stevens Publishing's list of high-quality books and multimedia programs, call 1-800-542-2595 (USA) or 1-800-461-9120 (Canada). Gareth Stevens Publishing's Fax: (414) 225-0377.
See our catalog, too, on the World Wide Web: http://gsinc.com

Library of Congress Cataloging-in-Publication Data

Ethan, Eric.
   Firebirds / by Eric Ethan.
     p. cm. — (Great American muscle cars—an imagination library series.
   Includes index.
   Summary: Surveys the history of the Pontiac Firebird and its designs, engines, performance, and costs.
   ISBN 0-8368-1745-1 (lib. bdg.)
   1. Firebird automobile—Juvenile literature. [1. Firebird automobile.] I. Title. II. Series: Ethan, Eric. Great American muscle cars—an imagination library series.
TL215.F57E84   1998
629.222'2—dc21   97-41183

First published in North America in 1998 by
Gareth Stevens Publishing
1555 North RiverCenter Drive, Suite 201
Milwaukee, WI 53212 USA

This edition © 1998 by Gareth Stevens, Inc. Text by Eric Ethan. Photographs by Ron Kimball (cover, page 9) and Nicky Wright (pages 5, 7, 11, 13, 15, 17, 19, and 21). Additional end matter © 1998 by Gareth Stevens, Inc.

Text: Eric Ethan
Page layout: Eric Ethan, Helene Feider
Cover design: Helene Feider
Series design: Shari Tikus

Printed in the United States of America

1 2 3 4 5 6 7 8 9 02 01 00 99 98

TABLE OF CONTENTS

Words that appear in the glossary are printed in **boldface** type the first time they occur in the text.

THE FIRST FIREBIRD

   Firebirds are made by the Pontiac division of General Motors. The first Firebird was built in mid-1967. It was the last of the great American muscle cars manufactured during the 1960s.

   General Motors is a large carmaker in Detroit, Michigan. Besides Pontiacs, General Motors also makes Chevrolets. The most famous Chevrolet muscle cars of the 1960s were the Corvette and Camaro. Firebirds and Camaros were based on the same basic **design**. General Motors saved money by using the same parts in both cars.

*Muscle cars are American-made, two-door sports **coupes** with powerful engines made for high-performance driving. The 1969 Pontiac Firebird Trans Am muscle car pictured shows the classic lines of the Firebird.*

WHAT DO FIREBIRDS LOOK LIKE?

Firebirds and Camaros looked very much alike at first. Both had long hoods and short rear decks. These features were found in a class of autos called *Pony cars*. Pony cars got their nickname from the Ford Mustang. The Mustang was the most popular car of its type during the 1960s.

Firebirds and Camaros shared a smooth body design. The round lines over the wheels and passenger **compartment** were similar to European designs of the time. But designers at Chevrolet and Pontiac worked hard to make their cars look different from the European versions. Each car had its own list of available **options**.

A long hood and short rear deck were common to all Pony cars, including this 1967 Firebird.

WHAT WAS THE FASTEST FIREBIRD?

Firebird customers could choose what engine size they wanted. The smallest engines were not very fast. Many people wanted Firebirds with bigger and faster engines that could produce 300 **horsepower** or more.

The fastest Firebird was also the last of these powerful muscle cars ever made. By 1972, production of big-motor muscle cars slowed. It was a surprise in 1973 when Pontiac began making a limited number of Firebirds with an SD-455 motor and 375 horsepower. The SD-455 used a large amount of gasoline. It was very powerful and very loud. This Firebird could easily reach over 125 miles (200 kilometers) per hour — the fastest Firebird of all.

Firebird's 1969 400 convertible was one of the fastest factory-made muscle cars of that year.

FIREBIRD ENGINES

The SD-455 was the biggest engine Pontiac ever put into a Firebird. After the mid-1970s, Firebirds came with smaller engines that emphasized **fuel economy** and **pollution** control instead of high performance.

In the early 1990s, Pontiac **engineers** again began to design powerful engines. But these looked much different from the big V-8 motors in the muscle cars of the 1960s. Newer high-performance Pontiac motors have a lot of **emission** control equipment on them. They are powerful, but they don't use a lot of gasoline or pollute the air like the cars of the 1960s did.

This 1992 Pontiac Formula Trans Am high-performance engine features a large amount of emission control equipment that is now standard on American cars.

11

FIREBIRD INTERIORS

Pontiac's newest Firebirds offer the same passenger compartment features found in muscle cars of the 1960s. Bucket seats and the center console **stick shift** are standard.

By the 1990s, seat belts were required. Early muscle cars sometimes did not have seat belts or other safety equipment that is common today. Today's Firebirds even have air bags.

Pontiac's 1992 version of the Formula Trans Am has bucket seats and a center console stick shift similar to those first introduced in Firebirds of the 1960s.

13

FIREBIRDS RACING

Both Chevrolet and Ford made special racing models of their cars to promote their regular models. But Pontiac did not promote its cars in this way. Some Firebirds did do well, however, in **Trans Am road races**. For these races, Pontiac borrowed Chevrolet's Z-28 engine made for Camaros. Firebirds that used the engines did well, but there were few of them.

Most racing Firebirds were owned by individuals who bought the car with the powerful SD-455 motor. They entered these Firebirds in **drag races**. The heavy but powerful SD-455 motor made the Firebird a winner.

The 1970 Firebird Trans Am has a super-duty 455-cubic-inch (7.5-liter) engine capable of very high speeds on long, straight tracks.

BEAUTIFUL FIREBIRDS

The basic Firebird design did not change very much during its first three years. Firebirds were popular with new-car buyers, and Pontiac wanted to stick with a winner. Most of the design changes were to trim the front bumper area. The 1969 model had the front bumper and grill designed into the rest of the body. This emphasized the long hood and overall sleek lines.

The Trans Am model Firebird had special styling options added. These included large air **spoilers** below the front bumper and wheel wells.

Many collectors believe the 1969 Firebirds like the convertible pictured combined the best design elements of all the models from the 1960s.

THE LAST FIREBIRDS

The last really powerful Firebirds were made in 1976. That was the final year a Firebird could be ordered with an SD-455 motor. By 1976, all other American carmakers had long since stopped putting powerful engines into their cars. Many people were concerned about the amount of gasoline bigger engines used and the pollution they caused. Fast cars were also more dangerous to drive.

After 1976, Firebirds became slower and safer, and they are still made today. The design has changed a great deal over the years.

The Firebird design has changed greatly over time as shown by this 1994 Formula Firebird.

19

WHAT DID ORIGINAL FIREBIRDS COST?

Firebirds were a bargain when they were first manufactured. Pontiac offered a long list of options so customers could make their Firebird unique. The options included bigger motors and special tires.

Options added to the price of a new Firebird. But even when the best options were ordered, it was still difficult to spend more than $4,000 on the car. As a result of low pricing and quality, Firebirds sold well.

This 1969 Firebird convertible cost less than $3,000 when it was new.

21

WHAT DO FIREBIRDS COST TODAY?

Over 400,000 Firebirds were sold between 1967 and 1973. During those years, the fastest and most popular muscle car versions were made. Many of these original cars still exist.

The most valuable of the original Firebirds are well **preserved** or **restored** with large motors and special speed equipment. Collectors are willing to pay many times the original price for Firebirds that are fully restored. Prices for some of the rarest SD-455 models are well over $10,000. Even so, this is still a bargain among muscle cars from the 1960s.

GLOSSARY

compartment (kom-PART-ment) — A separate area surrounded by four walls or sides.

coupe (koop) — An enclosed, two-door automobile for usually two people that is normally smaller than a sedan.

design (dee-ZINE) — The plans and specifications for a new product.

drag race — An acceleration contest between cars over a course that is in a straight line.

emission (ee-MISH-ehn) — A condition during which substances are discharged into the air.

engineer (ehn-jin-EER) — In the automobile industry, a person who designs and builds engines.

fuel economy (FU-el ee-CON-oh-me) — A rating that reveals how far a vehicle can travel on a certain amount of gasoline or other fuel, and therefore its fuel efficiency.

horsepower (HORS pow-er) — A system for measuring engine ability based on the amount of weight one horse can pull.

option (OP-shun) — A feature that can be added over and above the regular features.

pollution (poh-LU-shun) — Wastes and poisons that enter the air, land, and water.

preserve (pre-ZERVE) — To keep intact and free of decay.

restore (ree-STORE) — To fix an item so that it becomes like new.

spoiler (SPOYL-er) — A small lip on an automobile. When a car is traveling fast, a spoiler will push the car down toward the road for safer handling.

stick shift (STIHK shift) — The manually operated gearshift of an automobile.

Trans Am road race (tranz AM) — A car race on special curved tracks that is set up by the Sports Car Club of America.

WEB SITES

www.inlink.com/~jwinkler/

www.pontiac.com/

www.classicar.com/clubs/natfireb

www.tatribe.com

134407

PLACES TO WRITE

Classic Motorbooks
729 Prospect Avenue, P.O. Box 1
Osceola, WI 54020 1-800-826-6600

High Performance Pontiac
McMullen and Argus Publishing
774 South Placentia Avenue
Placentia, CA 92870-6832

National Firebird Club
P.O. Box 11238
Chicago, IL 60611

Pontiac Enthusiast
P.O. Box 6489
Orange, CA 92613-6489

INDEX